Sing Praise

The Lord delights in those who revere him,
in those who wait for his love.

Psalm 146

The Benedictine Nuns
of Turvey Abbey

McCrimmons
Great Wakering Essex England

First published in United Kingdom in 2001 by
McCRIMMON PUBLISHING CO LTD
10-12, High Street, Great Wakering, Essex SS3 0EQ
Telephone: 01702 218956
Fax: 01702 216082
Email: mccrimmons@dial.pipex.com
Web site: www.mccrimmons.com

ISBN 0 85597 631 4

Other titles in the series

Jesus, Our Light   ISBN 0 85597 611 X
Jesus, Our Hope   ISBN 0 85597 612 8
Jesus, Our Way   ISBN 0 85597 613 6
God's Promises   ISBN 0 85597 620 9

All images are taken from original paintings by the Benedictine
Nuns of Turvey Abbey, part of the *Old Testament series* of posters.
Design and Layout Alan Hencher
Typeset in Frutiger Light 11.5/13.5pt, 10/12pt and
ITC Fenice Regular Italic 24/26pt
Printed by Thanet Press Ltd, Margate, Kent, United Kingdom

Contents

Sing Praise!
The Psalms

The set of posters which accompany this book depict extracts from twelve of the Psalms. starting with Psalm 1 – True happiness, through to Psalm 150 – Praise the Lord.

Using this booklet

This booklet is designed to help teachers, catechists, R.E. co-ordinators and others to make the most of these beautiful images. On each page the artist has sought to describe her inspiration for each painting by reflecting on the relevant scripture references. We have also included:

- a picture of the poster;

- paraphrased text of the psalm for children

- questions for discussion.

Discussion and teaching

The Questions for Discussion included in this booklet are designed to help teachers and catechists develop the responses of children to these well-known Psalms. If you have time, we suggest you look up the scriptural reference yourself and reflect on it. Why not use a piece of the text as a heading for a display or a starting point for a session? We do not aim to offer formulaic lessons and hope you will adapt and alter the material to suit the needs of the children in your care.

Display and decoration

The vibrant and striking colours of the paintings means they are ideally suited to display in Church, on notice-boards, as the centre piece of an R.E. display or prayer table/altar, or around school. You may wish to copy or type out one or more of the Questions for Discussion on each page and arrange them with the poster/s to make your displays more interactive and appealing to children and adults alike.

Assemblies and services

The posters are ideal for use in assemblies and services. You may want to display them as a basis for discussion or as a stimulus for prayer or reflection. They will also add colour and meaning to Bible stories read or acted out in the parish or school.

Prayer and meditation

A striking visual image often helps people to pray, meditate or reflect. You could use one or more of the posters as a focal point for an altar/prayer table or as the centre piece of a prayer service.

Creative writing and artwork

The rich and vivid colour of these illustrations, combined with the powerful imagery, makes them an ideal starting point for creative work. Why not use them to provoke thought and discussion before writing poetry or prayers? Or how about asking children to copy or re-design an image as part of their art work?

And finally...

Why not share your ideas and experiences with us?

We are always interested in finding out what works well and what materials you need to better fulfil your ministry.

Contact us at::
McCRIMMONS, Freepost CL2425,
Southend-on-Sea, Essex, SS3 0BR.
Tel: (01702) 218956 Fax (01702) 216082
email: mccrimmons@dial.pipex.com
www.mccrimmons.com

You will be happy if you follow God's ways.
Learn about God and try to follow him.

If you follow God's ways,
you will be like a tree planted by a stream.
You will produce lots of good fruit.

God looks after those who follow him.
But those who turn their back on God
will be like chaff in the wind,
lost and blown away.

Psalm 1
True happiness

The Psalter opens with the image of the fruit-bearing tree standing by the waterside, striking a parallel with the tree of Life which opens Genesis, and going a step further, the tree of the cross which bore Jesus, the most precious fruit, the eating of which makes us become like him.

The flowing waters are our Baptism, the Gifts of the Spirit. The measure of our fruit-bearing will depend on our remaining rooted in Christ, the Source of Living waters. In the background sin is blown away life winnowed chaff on the storm of the Spirit. The psalm brings us the mystery of salvation in a nutshell.

Questions for discussion

1. This is the first psalm.
There are 150 altogether. Do you know any other psalms?

2. This psalm tells us about a tree and how it grows strong. What does a tree need to grow strong?
What do you need to grow strong?

3. A good friend of God is like a tree that grows strong. What sort of things can help us to grow in our friendship with God?

4. Do you know any good friends of God?
Can they help you?

Oh God you are wonderful,
the whole world sings your praise.
When I look up into the sky
I know that you are very powerful.

You put the moon and the stars in heaven
so that everybody would know how wonderful you are.
You made human beings and loved them so much
that you put them in charge of the earth

You gave us every creature that we can imagine
and trusted that we would care for them all.
Oh God you are wonderful,
the whole world sings your praise.

Psalm 8
God's glory and man's dignity

This psalm has the freshness and simplicity of the pure-in-heart, discovering the greatness and the beauty of God in the universe and breaking into a spontaneous song of praise. The theme suggests a simple, almost primitive treatment, to mirror the world-view of a child, a compact world of goodness and innocence, with children and animals and the fruits of the earth all praising the creator in the comforting presence of the caring grown-ups. A psalm reflecting an unspoiled paradise, the early beginnings when God saw that all that he had made was very good.

Questions for discussion

1. Do you have a favourite part of the psalm? Why?
Have you ever looked at the night sky? Close your eyes now and imagine a sky filled with stars.
What do you think this tells us about God?

2. God has put us in char ge of the whole of creation. How can you help to look after all that God has made?

3. The psalm praises God. How would you praise God in your own words?

Just look up into the sky,
you will see how wonderful our God is.
When we see the sun rise and the sun set
we know that you are a mighty God.

You made the powerful sun
no-one can escape from its heat,
we know that you are a mighty God.

God you are mighty,
you show us how to live.
If we follow your ways
we will be happy.

We want to follow your ways
we know that you will reward all our trying.
We will try our best.

You know all the things I think about
help me to be good.
You are mighty God,
you are my rescuer, my rock.

Psalm 18 (19)
David's song of victory

Like Psalm 8, this psalm begins with a burst of joyful wonder at the greatness of God evident in his creation. The poster shows the rounding of the globe where the sun is rising and setting, while in the heat of the day the fullness of the Spirit is poured out on the earth's inhabitants. The second half of the psalm magnifies the Law of the Lord. What is this law? The greatest commandment: Love. It is shown here as the unity of all peoples, the colours of the figures symbolising all races and creeds, united in loving each other and our one God and Father, the fullness of happiness in heaven and on earth, "more to be desired than gold."

Questions for discussion

1. We know how wonderful God is when we look at Creation. God tells us this without using words.
What is the most beautiful place you have ever visited?

2. Imagine that you have met someone who has never heard of God. You want to show them how wonderful God is but you can't use words. What would you show them?

3. This psalm tells us that God's law is perfect. What do you think God's laws are?

4. The person in this psalm promises to try his best in all that he thinks and does. How do you think that you can do your best today?

God you are like a shepherd,
you give me all that I need.
You feed me,
you help me when things are hard.

You show me the right path,
you keep me safe.
I don't need to be afraid.
You are always there.

When I'm frightened and no one is my friend
you let me know that I am special.
You have chosen me
you will always look after me.

I know that your love and kindness
will be with me forever.
I will always be a good friend of God.

Psalm 22 (23)
The Lord is my shepherd

Sheep today are safely kept from straying by wire fences and securely locked gates, with no shepherd in sight. In Biblical times the image of the shepherd who was ready to die for his sheep had powerful connotations, generating a complete trust in the shepherd's care and reliability, and it is this sense of trust which dominates the psalm. The emphasis is on the intimate relationship between the shepherd and each sheep personally. "The Lord is MY shepherd": the deep truth that he is there for me, I am unique to him; his individual attention and love are totally for every single one of his countless creatures. He knows each one by their name and they know him. Here too the refreshing waters are an image of the Spirit, and the psalm ends with the prophetic vision of the Eucharistic Banquet which the shepherd prepares for his sheep, with the overflowing cup of salvation, his very life which he lays down for them.

Questions for discussion

1. Have you ever seen a shepherd looking after sheep?

2. What do you think you need to be good at to be a shepherd?

3. God loves and looks after us just like a shepherd looks after his sheep. How do you know that God is looking after you.

4. Think of people who take care of you. Write your own psalm about all the things they do for you.

Help me God,
things are going very wrong.
I feel as if I'm drowning,
there's water everywhere.

Waves are crashing over my head.
My enemies are everywhere,
nobody is telling the truth.

God, you know what I have done
Please help me.

It does not matter what I try to do
people laugh and make fun of me.
I don't seem to have any friends.
Please answer me, God of love.

You are always there to help me,
save me now.

Please don't hide from me.
I will always sing your praise,
I know you listen to my cries.
The whole of the earth joins with my cries
please hear me.

Psalm 68 (69)
A cry for help

The Psalter records the whole gamut of human experience; here it is the S.O.S. of a drowning man in his agony, a scream of utter distress. He still has the presence of mind to voice his despair in a piercing cry to the God who alone can save him. This is the message of the psalm: God saves. It is shown by the hand surrounded by light which reaches into the deep, ready to grasp him, in spite of his understandable but hardly Christian feelings of revenge. The psalm ends on a note of relief and a song of praise and thanksgiving.

Questions for discussion

1. This psalm is about a man who was very frightened. Everything seems to be going wrong. Have you ever been very frightened?

2. The man in this psalm calls to God to help him? Who would you call if you needed help? Do you ever call God if you feel afraid?

3. At the end of the psalm the man says that he knows that God will look after those who need him. How do you know that God looks after you?

Oh God you are everywhere
you fill the earth with your love.
I want to be in your presence always.

Birds and animals feel safe in your presence
I want to sing your praise forever.
When people praise you they are happy,
even when times are difficult.

Oh God, please hear my prayer,
listen to the things I say.
Look down on our world
and keep us safe.

Oh God, your strength is like a shield
you will always protect us.
You will look after those who follow you
those who trust in you will always be happy.

Psalm 83 (84)
Longing for God's house

The Temple of Jerusalem was the great centre of the Chosen People's life and worship, the place where God lived among them, the symbol of their heavenly home. For us it stands for the Church, God's Kingdom on earth, the world-wide community of all who are incorporated in Christ. "There are many rooms in my Father's house", Jesus said. This House is shown here as a city of a great variety of dwellings where all find their home, even the swallows and sparrows, for did not St Paul assure us that all creation will share in the glory and freedom of God's children? Here too the waters of the Spirit are awash around the city, he who makes the bitter valley into a place of springs, and causes us to walk with ever growing strength.

Questions for discussion

1. This psalm tells us about the Temple in Jerusalem.
The person who wrote the psalm liked to go and pray in the Temple. Where do you like to pray

2. Some animals have made their home in the Temple.
They like to be close to God.
Where do you feel close to God?

3. The psalm tells us that God is our shield.
He will always look after us. When do you feel safe?

God you are wonderful !
We praise you.

You made the heavens
just like a very big tent.
You made clouds, wind and
   lightning
and all of these obey you.

You made the solid earth
and the deep, deep seas.
You made the highest mountain
and the very deepest valley.
God, you are wonderful!

You made streams in the valleys
   and hills
and all your animals can drink.
You make it rain so that things
   can grow
and we can have good things
   to eat.

You made the moon and the sun,
you fill the earth with darkness
   and it is night.
In the darkness wild animals
   come out.
You look after them all.

The things you have made fill
   the whole world.
You are a wonderful God.
The deep seas are full of your
   creatures
tiny fish and huge sea monsters.

You look after everything,
   great and small.
You never forget about any of
   your creatures.

If you forget about us for a
   moment
we would die and be dust again.
But you give us your love
and the whole earth is filled
   with life.

God you are wonderful
I want to sing your praise.
Praise the Lord for ever!

Psalm 103 (104)
In praise of the creator

This psalm looks like a poetic development of the brief and sober account of creation of the book of Genesis. Here a human being is overwhelmed by the beauty and wonder of it all and sings out his delight in glowing terms. Following him in his exploration we join him in thanksgiving, recognising God's guiding and sustaining hand in the mysterious workings of nature and of grace, of love in response to love, urging us to sing to him "all our lives, make music to our God while we live," our lives lived in harmony with our song.

Questions for discussion

1. This psalm tells us that the whole of creation shows us how wonderful God is God has power over everything that has been created. Where can you see God's power in the world?

2. God has created the world so that all creatures have what they need. What do you think this tells us about God?

3. The psalm tells us that there is a place for all of God's creatures. How do you think that we can make sure that there is a place for all living creatures today? What can we do to make sure that the world is a safe place for all living creatures.

Oh God you saved us from slavery,
We could hardly believe it.
We were so happy,
we laughed and we sang.

You are a mighty God.
Even the people who don't know you
said that you are mighty.

Let us always live in freedom
let us be like streams in the desert.
Let us trust in God in the hard times
and good times will be sure to come.
Sadness has turned to happiness.
People planted their fields and they cried
but now their arms are full of sheaves of wheat,
Everybody is happy.

Psalm 125 (126)
A prayer for deliverance

One of the "Psalms of Ascent" or "Pilgrim Songs", it was sung as the people went up to the holy mountain of Jerusalem, remembering how their ancestors had joyfully returned to their homeland after the Exile. The exile had been a painful experience, a 'sowing in tears' which had however greatly enhanced the joy of the return. In the climate of the Middle East harvesting occurs in spring, at the time of the Passover, when the first sheaves were presented in the Temple and the new, still unleavened bread was welcomed with great joy. We see here both sowers and harvesters in action, and in the ' streams in dry land' we can see the power of the Holy Spirit who brought the harvest about. We too have to become 'new, unleavened bread of sincerity and truth' (1 Corinthians 5:8) producing all the fruits of the Spirit (Galatians 5:22).

Questions for discussion

1. The psalm tells us of a difficult time for God's chosen people. They had to go and live in a strange land called Babylon. The people were very unhappy. Have you ever had to live somewhere strange? How did it feel?

2. God saved his people and they were able to go back to their own country. The people were so happy to be back in their own country. They sang and praised God. What sort of things would make you want to sing and praise God?

3. God really did a great thing for his people. Can you think of any other stories in the Bible where God did something for his people?

4. The psalm tells us that the people tried to plough the land but the land was hard. Their work was hard and they felt sad. Is your work ever hard?

5. The people had to trust God that things would get easier. What do you do when life seems hard?

We thank you God
you will always love us.

God you have done wonderful
    things.
You made the skies and the earth
and all the mighty seas.

You will always love us.

It was you who made the sun
    and the stars
and the moon that shines in the
    night.

You will always love us.

You saved your chosen people
and set them free from slavery.

You will always love us.

You made a path through the
    Red sea
and your people came to dry
    land,
but the Egyptians and their
    horses drowned in the sea.

You will always love us.

You showed your people the
    way in the desert
and you saved them from their
    enemies.

You will always love us.

Your people came to live in a
    new country
you looked after them all of the
    time.

You will always love us.

No enemies could harm your
    people.
You give food to everything that
    lives.
We thank you God of the whole
    world.

We know that you will always
    love us.

Psalm 135 (136)
Give thanks to the Lord

This litany of God's love for his people repeating after each verse its joyful refrain, is like a mantra of praise and thanksgiving. The whole story of God's great deeds for his people is brought together here, from the Big Bang of creation right down to his ultimate act of salvation when he will be all in all. The poster follows this story: creation, salvation, struggle, victory, fulfilment, in the images of the Old Testament history, typical of the realities of our own daily lives. The white figure at the end stands for redeemed humanity having reached the Promised Land.

Questions for discussion

1. This psalm tells us the story of how God created the world, how he saved his people and how he looks after all that he has made. How do you know that God has looked after you from the time that you were born until now?

2. The Psalm says that God's love will never end. What does this tell us about God?

3. Do you have a favourite part of this Psalm? Why?

4. Make a list of five things that you would like to thank God for.

O Lord, you know everything
 about me.
You know when I get up and
 when I go to sleep.
You know what I am going to do
 next.

You know what I am going to say
 before I say it
you are very close to me.
You look after me wherever I am
you are closer than I can ever
 imagine.

Your presence is everywhere.
If I climbed a very high
 mountain
or dug deep into the ground
you would still be by my side.

If I could fly far away
as far as the end of the sea
you would still be there
looking after me.

Even when it's very dark
you stay close to me.
There is nowhere that I can hide
 from you.

You made me
and kept me safe inside my
 mum.
Thank you for making me
and everything in the world.

Before I was born you knew all
 about me.
Everything about me was a
 secret that only you knew.
You loved every part of me
 before I was born.

Oh God you are wonderful.
You are a mystery to me.

God keep me safe beside you.
Don't let any enemies attack me.
If people are your enemies they
 are my enemies too.

Oh God stay close to me and
 everything that I think.
Make sure that I always follow
 your plan for me
that I always follow the way
 that leads to you.

Psalm 138 (139)
Lord, you have examined me and you know me

Every human heart in search of God will find its own journey echoed in this psalm. Intuition, longing, delight, bafflement, fear, despair, flight and frustration, return and surrender are beautifully expressed in this poem, which also reflects St Augustine's cry 'Our hearts are restless until they rest in you.' A wonderful theme for pictorial representation: we follow the psalmist from his first awakening until his final surrender and fulfilment.

Questions for discussion

1. Look carefully at the picture.
Do you have a favourite part?

2. The psalm tells us that wherever you go, God will always be with you. Talk about the times and places when you know that God is with you.

3. God knows everything that we think and do.
He knows the things that are precious to us.
What is precious to you?

Sing praise to God because he is good.
Sing praise to God because he loves us.
Everybody wants to praise God.

God you made Jerusalem into a great city again.
We thought everything was spoiled.
You led your people to safety.
You look after the sick and even those who are sad.

You filled the sky with stars
and gave each one a name.
Oh God you are so strong and wise.
You can do anything.
Sing praise to God!

You fill the sky with clouds
and send us the rain we need.
You help our plants to grow
and we have enough to eat.
You give food to all your animals
even the ravens can call on you for help.

God you are pleased when we love you
when we put all our trust in you.

Psalm 146 (147)
In praise of God the Almighty

This song has the quality of a fairy tale, the narrator jumping from the sparkling city of Jerusalem to the misery of the poor and needy and the sick, and from there to the splendour of the skies, clouds and rain God's gift to the earth, its people and its animals. In the Hebrew text psalms 146 and 147 are one, adding further fairy tale like touches, the rigours and the beauty of winter, and finally a great cry of wonder: He has not dealt thus with other nations! Today we know that he has: Good News is for all nations.

Questions for discussion

1. This psalm tells us that God is very powerful. God uses his power to help us. Do you know any stories in the Bible where God uses his power.

2. The psalm tells us to put our trust in God. Can you think of a time when you have needed to trust in God?

3. The psalms speaks about the things that God can do for his people. What would you like God to do for you?

4. The psalm tells us to thank God for all that he has done. Think of three things that you would like to thank God for.

Everybody praise God!
Praise him everywhere,
Praise him in heaven and on earth.
Let's praise him for the wonderful things he has done.

Praise God with trumpets, lutes and harps.
Let's bang drums and dance
lets play the flute and the violin.

Let's clash enormous cymbals
and be as loud as we can!
Everybody, everywhere
let's tell God how much we love him!!!!

Psalm 150
Praise the Lord!

As the Psalter started with the image of the fruit-bearing tree from the first book of the Bible, so it ends anticipating the praise and glory of the last book, the Book of Revelation, with its great throngs of angels and saints proclaiming the final victory of God and of the Lamb. With the Psalmist we are still looking forward to that completion, in anticipated joy promised to us by Christ. With the psalm we live in that joy, expressed here in a dance of musicians sounding their instruments, in colour and movement, 'all that lives and breathes' joining in. Praise engenders joy, joy engenders praise. A psalm to make our daily prayer.

Questions for discussion

1. This is the last psalm in the book of Psalms. The psalm tells us to praise God wherever we are. Talk about all the different places in which we can praise God.

2. The writer calls us to praise God for all of the wonderful things that he has done. make a list of all the things that God has done for the people in your class or parish.

3. Read the psalm again and see how many musical instruments you can count.

4. If you could praise God with any instrument what would it be.?

Meditation with children

The use of traditional meditation techniques with children can provide an important opportunity for spiritual development. The images in this book, and the associated posters, can be used as the stimulus for reflection. Each image is the fruit of many years of meditation by the artist herself and the shapes, colours and textures of each painting draw us powerfully into the Gospel scene. By offering children an opportunity to explore the work of this artist we are giving them one way to make the Gospel come alive.

Each meditation, appearing on the left hand side from page 6-28, can be read by the teacher or group leader. They have been designed to be read slowly, pausing for a short time at appropriate points to give children time to reflect.

Here are some simple guidelines for meditating with children:

1 Location
choose a peaceful area, preferably a room where the door can be closed;
make sure the area is sufficiently large and comfortable.

2 Timing
establish a routine and stick to it;
particularly suitable times include the beginning and end of the day;
avoid times of general excitement in the school or parish.

3 Stimulus
choose a stimulus that has obvious appeal to the senses;
make sure you have gathered and organised your resources well before the session;
consider using music, periods of silence or objects to help set the scene.

4   Focus

a lighted candle provides a simple focus;
arrange your objects, including the poster, carefully to ensure they
are not disturbed.

5   Openness

try to be as relaxed as possible;
don't force a situation. If something is a disaster, abandon it!

Preparation

Arrange the room with the poster as a focal point. You may light a candle
and place it near the poster. Help the children to become still by
encouraging them to sit in an upright position. Suggest they close their
eyes and rest hands in their laps. The following routine may help children
or adults to centre themselves:

Sit as still as you can and listen carefully to all the sounds around you. Can
you hear anything outside? Listen to it for a while, then try to let it go.
Breathe gently and slowly, in and out. Imagine you are in the room by
yourself. When you are ready, open your eyes and look at the picture in
front of you.

Look first at all the different colours. Are they happy or sad? Angry or
peaceful? How would you describe them? Close your eyes and see how
many colours from the picture you can remember. Now look at the shapes
that have been used. How do they make you feel? Do you like the picture?
Imagine that the artist is sitting right beside you. Tell her what you think.
Do you know the story? Do you know what happens next?

The meditations under the pictures in this book are a guidance intended
to help children enter into the scene depicted by the poster. They need not
be used word for word. Some children will find it difficult to sustain
concentration during this type of activity and may need reassurance.

Concluding meditation

Allow some time at the end of the session for children to give feedback if
they wish. You may want to use the Questions for Discussion on each
page. Some children may find it difficult to give verbal feedback
immediately. Perhaps you could provide materials for them to record their
responses in words or drawings.

Jesus, Our Life poster series
THE BENEDICTINE NUNS OF TURVEY ABBEY

Part 2 **Jesus, Our Way**

The next step in this exciting and highly acclaimed poster series shows us the way Jesus leads us – through suffering and death to the glory of the Resurrection and the coming of the Holy Spirit. Twelve posters suitable for use at Lent & Easter.

12 Full colour laminated posters / Size: A2 / Ref: LOC2P

Part 3 **Jesus, Our Hope**

In this set of posters based on the Life of Jesus, we follow the Ministry of Our lord in the colourful depictions of his miracles, parables and others events, which build our faith and lead us in hope.

12 Full colour laminated posters / Size: A2 / Ref: LOC3P

God's Promise

A set of posters illustrating the power of the Old Testament. Starting at Genesis with a vibrant depiction of God's Creation and on to God's Blessing to Abraham and his people. Exodus follows with Moses receiving the Ten Commandments and then to Joshua and the story of the Promised Land. This colourful poster set carries on to illustrate some more of the fascinating stories from Scripture.

12 Full colour laminated posters / Size: A2 / Ref: POT1

1 **Breath of the Spirit**
2 **Spirit Alive**
SISTER SHEILA GOSNEY

Two striking sets of posters. The first is an ideal resource for confirmation programmes, the second expresses the external imagery of the Holy Spirit – Fire, Wind and Water the Dove – and other symbols of the life of the Christian church. Each poster, with the help of an accompanying booklet, may be used to explore the messages of the Scriptures.

Breath of the Spirit
8 Full colour laminated posters and guide booklet / Size: A2 / Ref: MPCP1
Spirit Alive
8 Full colour laminated posters and guide booklet / Size: A2 / Ref: MPSA

The Footsteps of Christ
THE BENEDICTINE NUNS OF TURVEY ABBEY

This popular set has been created from 16 glorious oil paintings by the Benedictine Nuns of Turvey Abbey. Suitable for Lent & Easter, the posters follow Christ along the journey of the Cross from Peter's denial to the entombment and ending with the joy and hope of the resurrection.

16 Full colour laminated posters (includes FREE book) / Size: A2 / Ref: FOCP